Your Dog, You,

and the

Pandemic!

Ways to Survive Together
Without Losing Your Mind

Sherri Cappabianca, CSAMP, CSAAP

Certified Small Animal Massage Practitioner
Certified Small Animal Acupressure Practitioner

Off The Leash Press, LLC

OffTheLeashPress.com

Your Dog, You, and the Pandemic!: *Ways to Survive Together Without Losing Your Mind*
by Sherri Cappabianca (with Rik Feeney)

This book is intended as a reference to help dog owners navigate being confined at home with a dog who is also confined. It is not intended to diagnose, advise, or treat any condition, nor is it a replacement for regular veterinary care. The author and publisher assume no liability in connection with use of the information presented in this book.

ISBN: 978-0-9841982-2-1 (paperback)
         978-0-9841982-4-5 (Kindle)

Off the Leash Press, LLC
119 Lucky Dog Ln.
Hendersonville, NC
info@offtheleashpress.com
OffTheLeashPress.com

Cover Design / Formatting & Edited by:
Rik Feeney www.RickFeeney.com

Cover photo:
Dana Brooks

Interior photos:
Sherri Cappabianca or Big Stock Photo (bigstockphoto.com)

Contents

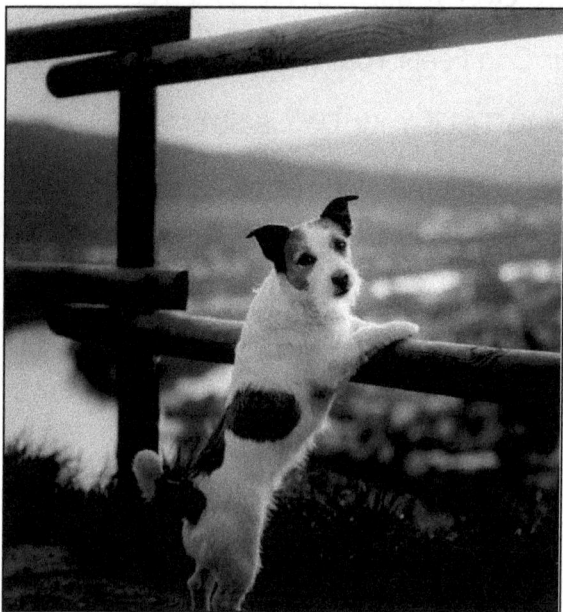

CHAPTER 1
We're Over It, but It's Not Over Yet!

Life has definitely changed for all of us over the last couple of months, since "shelter in place" was ordered by the government. And who knew "social distancing" would become the defining phrase of 2020? Unless we work for an essential business, we've been stuck at home for several weeks now. And the stress is starting to show for many of us.

Yes, we can go out to get groceries and other essentials, and in some places we can take a walk, but I think we all miss the things we used to take for granted – going shopping, out to eat, kids in school, and more.

We are social animals and until recently have taken for granted seeing our friends whenever we want, going out for entertainment, seeing and hugging our parents, children, siblings, and other family members. We are in essence suffering from separation anxiety, much like some dogs do when we leave to go to work for the day.

Just as we feel the effects of sheltering in place and social distancing, our dogs feel the same. Many dogs experience stress, which can manifest as seeming depression, loss of appetite, lethargy, or destructive behavior.

Dogs are Social Animals, Too!

Dogs are social animals just like humans, and many are feeling the loss of their social activities, such as going to doggy daycare, the dog park, or meeting up with friends for a play date. Just like with children, we have to engage our dogs in different ways now. And we need to rely on them more than ever to give us that safe companionship we all need.

Life will be different for some time to come, depending on what happens with this virus. No one yet knows when or if we can go back to life as it was pre-pandemic. But once we can begin to resume normal activities, with social distancing precautions, we will still need to be cautious of many of the activities we used to do with our dogs, such as going to the dog park, or meeting friends for a play date. Social distancing will still need to be top of mind, at least until it's safe to be in close contact with one another again.

CHAPTER 2
Your Dog Feels Your Pain

Not only can your dog feel anxious because his routine has been disrupted during this time, but he can also detect your anxiety as well. Dogs are naturally very observant, which is one way they learn the rules of the household. But it also means they can pick up on our emotions. How do they always seem to know when we need to pet them or cuddle with them?

Dogs intuitively know how we're feeling. They know our body language, our facial expressions, and the tone and frequency of our voices. They know when those change. Dogs that are close to you are likely able to tell if you are happy, sad, angry, anxious, and more. They can also sense chemical changes in our bodies, which is how they can detect things like cancer.

When we're anxious, our dogs tend to get anxious as well. They perceive a threat and naturally feel less safe. So if you notice your dog acting differently, seemingly stressed, have a close look at your own emotions.

How are you acting differently? What can you do to change your behavior and keep yourself calm? Whatever that is, be it more exercise, meditation, yoga, listening to music, sitting quietly petting your dog, or more, try to change your outlook for the health of both of you.

CHAPTER 3
How to Tell if Your Dog
is Stressed

Often it can be difficult to tell if your dog is stressed or anxious unless the anxiety is severe. Most dogs exhibit subtle signs most humans don't easily pick up on or don't pay attention to.

Even if you know your dog well, some of these behaviors can go unnoticed or can be mistaken for other behaviors.

For example, is your dog yawning because he's tired or because he's trying to calm himself down? A lot of that depends upon the situation. If it's bedtime, a yawn is likely because he's tired. On the other hand, if you're at the vet's office and your dog hates going, a yawn is his way of calming himself down.

Physical Signs of a Dog's Stress

So what are some of the signs your dog is stressed? Here are a few:

- Panting when he's not hot, or shivering when it's not cold.

- Attempting to remove himself from a situation or going off to hide somewhere.

- Whale eyes. This happens when your dog exposes the whites of his eyes.

- Ears pinned back or tail tucked. These are more obvious signs.

- Scratching or biting especially his paws, when he's not itchy.

- Excessive barking or whining.

- Destructive behaviors such as chewing up the carpet or a pillow.

- Having potty accidents in the house despite being house trained.

- Restlessness, pacing, or the inability to sit still and calm down.

- Lip licking.

- Avoiding eye contact or looking away.

Every dog is different, and some react to stress more intensely than others.

My dog, Fletcher, hardly reacts to most stressors while his best friend Henry is always on alert, hides under my friend's office desk or in her closet, and barks at most things he sees. We both adopted our dogs when they were two-years-old, and both had some sort of abuse in their previous homes. But the difference in the breed mix (Fletcher is a Goldendoodle, Irish wolfhound mix and Henry is a mountain feist, pointer mix - we think) cause them to react differently when put in stressful situations.

So pay attention to your dog and what he's trying to tell you, especially during this stressful time. If you would like ideas on ways to help reduce your dog's stress, read on.

CHAPTER 4
Ways to Reduce Your Dog's Stress

Reducing your dog's stress and anxiety levels is critical especially now. Unchecked anxiety can result in more serious behavior problems the longer the stress is present.

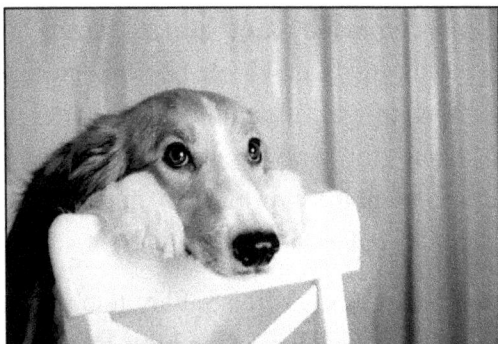

Your Dog, You, and the Pandemic!

There are a number of ways to help make sure your furry friend is as stress free as possible.

- Stick to a routine as much as possible. I'm sure most of us have experienced dramatic changes compared to our normal routines of going to work or school, going out with friends, picking the kids up from school, etc. Now that we are being told to stay home, that has completely changed.

  Even as states begin to open up slowly, we likely won't be back to what we previously considered normal for quite some time. Even in this "new normal" I'm sure by now you have some sort of routine. Stick to it by keeping life on a similar schedule each day. Your dog will learn what to expect - it will help reassure him and help keep him calm.

- Work on his mental stimulation by keeping up with his training. Teach him a new trick or command. Get him a puzzle toy that holds treats or kibble for him to figure out how to get. Or put peanut butter inside a Kong toy and freeze it. Most dogs will spend hours working to get all the peanut butter out.

- Keep up the exercise. Play fetch in the yard, or go for walks, something that is good for both of you. If you have a treadmill, teach your dog to walk on it. They can!

- Pay a lot more attention to your dog. Pet him often and spend time cuddling with him, even if it's in front of the TV.

- Try massaging your dog. If you don't know how, buy a book or try to find YouTube videos on the correct way to do a massage on an animal.

- For more anxious dogs, try CDB oil. It is reportedly effective in helping both humans and dogs who have anxiety. It's important however to do your research as all CBD products are not created equal.

- Feed your dog the best food you can afford to buy. Stress and anxiety affect the body negatively, and poor nutrition on top of that can bring on or compound health problems.

- Consider giving him a selection of real foods that help to manage stress. Some ideas are:

  o Blueberries – they provide a host of vitamins, minerals, and antioxidants that protect against the effects of stress.

o Kale – a great vegetable loaded with nutrients. Every day my dog Fletcher gets a vegetable mix that contains kale.

o Beef – preferably raw. It's a natural antidepressant.

o Turkey – again preferably raw. Turkey has L-tryptophan which is known to help with sleep and to calm humans and dogs down.

o Brown rice or whole oats – these need to be organic, because of glyphosate concerns. Both brown rice and whole oats help with the absorption of tryptophan.

o Almonds – they support healthy nerve function, helping the body better able to handle stress. Almond butter in a Kong is a great treat for any dog!

o Pumpkin seeds – another great source of L-tryptophan.

Your Dog, You, and the Pandemic!

Personally, I am not a fan of the so called "calming" kibble that some dog food companies are manufacturing. I think they're an overpriced gimmick and the ingredients aren't that great. If my dog was stressed, I would rather give him real food with real vitamins that his body can use to help reduce his stress. I urge you to do the same.

If your dog isn't acting like his normal self, try some of the suggestions above to see if one or more helps to manage his stress level. You will be rewarded with a healthier, happier companion.

CHAPTER 5
If You're Bored, so is Your Dog

Is everyone bored yet? Tired of binge watching Netflix? Have you read all the books in your library? Are the kids tired of their video games? It's not surprising that many people say they're bored after so many weeks of lockdown.

Chances are, if you're bored, so is your dog. Dogs are capable of becoming bored just like humans.

When we become bored with so much of the same thing, we typically don't engage with our dogs like we normally would. There's no energy to do so. I know when I get bored I don't feel like doing much of anything. We are a major source of our dogs' entertainment and when we don't feel like engaging them, they get bored.

Think back to when you would come home from work or school each day and your dog was there to excitedly greet you. I'm sure you were excited to see him too. You spent time engaging him. You played with him or took him for a walk.

Now, because you're together all the time, that aspect of missing your dog is gone. And likely, so is your motivation to do something with him.

Signs of a Bored Dog

Left to their own devices, bored dogs will make their own fun, most likely in ways that won't please you! Dogs that are bored exhibit their boredom in several different ways.

- They become destructive – such as chewing on inappropriate objects in the house, digging, excessively barking, and getting into things they shouldn't, like the trash.
- They seek constant attention, by barking or whining at you.
- They constantly follow you around the house, known as the Velcro Dog Syndrome.

Your Dog, You, and the Pandemic!

What should you do if you suspect your dog is bored? Try your best to motivate yourself out of your own boredom and do something with him. For ideas, read on!

CHAPTER 6
Fun Things You Can Do with Your Dog during Lockdown

Turning lockdown into as much of a game as possible can be a lot of fun for both you and your dog. I know many people who aren't able to go out of their homes right now, making it difficult to care for our dogs the way we normally would.

If you're stuck inside there are a number of training exercises and fun games you can play with your dog that will relieve boredom for both of you.

One of the most common games is tug-of-war. Most dogs love this game – it brings out their predatory drive. It's mentally and physically stimulating for your dog and can give you some fun and exercise too. I know there's controversy surrounding the game because some people believe it leads to aggressive behaviors. While I've never seen that happen, it's possible that it can, unless some basic rules are followed.

- The most important rule in playing tug-of-war is to teach your dog a release command, such as "drop it." This way, you can end the game should you need to.

- Always use a toy designed for playing tug-of-war, one that gives you both an end to pull on, and keeps your hand away from your dog's mouth.

- It's OK if your dog gets excited while playing tug-of-war, but keep the game from getting out of control. If it does, stop the game until your dog calms down.

- Stop the game immediately if you accidently get bit.

- Despite some beliefs to the contrary, you can let your dog win the game, but only as long as he is behaving appropriately. Any inappropriate behavior should result in the game being stopped immediately.

Another fun indoor game is "hide the toy or treats." I play this game with my dog using one of his favorite toys. Show your dog the toy he's supposed to find, let him sniff it, and then ask him to sit while you go hide the toy. Your dog should remain sitting in the room where you left him until you return from hiding the toy. Give him the command "find it" and off he goes from room to room looking until he finds the toy.

I always follow my dog as he searches, telling him to "find it" to encourage his search. Once he finds the toy, I give him lots of praise. This game is great fun, mentally challenging, works on reinforcing the sit/stay command, and is easy to play in the house.

You can also play chase or hide and seek from each other. Hide and seek is similar to hiding the toy, except this time you're the one that's hiding. You have to be a bit more careful with this game since you're running around the house, but it can give you and your dog a good workout on a day when you can't otherwise go outside.

Teach your dog some new tricks or commands. Most dogs love to learn new things. You can incorporate the new commands into something that will become his job going forward. Most working breeds need a job anyway, so now is a great time to do that. Teach him to fetch your shoes, or carry the groceries. My first golden retriever, Rocky, loved to carry groceries in from the car!

Set up a simple agility or exercise course in your home. Place pieces of furniture or other obstacles that your dog can go around, under, stand on, or jump over. Then work on training your dog to "run" the course. Change it up once he gets the hang of it.

You can also set up things like cushions, wood or plastic boxes, and whatever else you can find and have your dog walk on those. Walking on cushions and other uneven surfaces is great exercise both mentally and physically. Just a few minutes every day will go a long way to keeping your dog in good physical condition, and will relieve any potential boredom.

Try baking some dog treats. There are many recipes on the internet that are healthy and yummy. I'm sure your dog will love to be the taste tester! It's also a great time to reinforce training commands with those yummy treats as incentive!

If you are allowed to go out of the house and walk your dog, mix up the walk. Doing the same walk every day can become boring for him. Explore new streets and neighborhoods. Allow your dog to sniff these new surroundings; it provides mental stimulation. Plus it's great for you to experience new scenery as well.

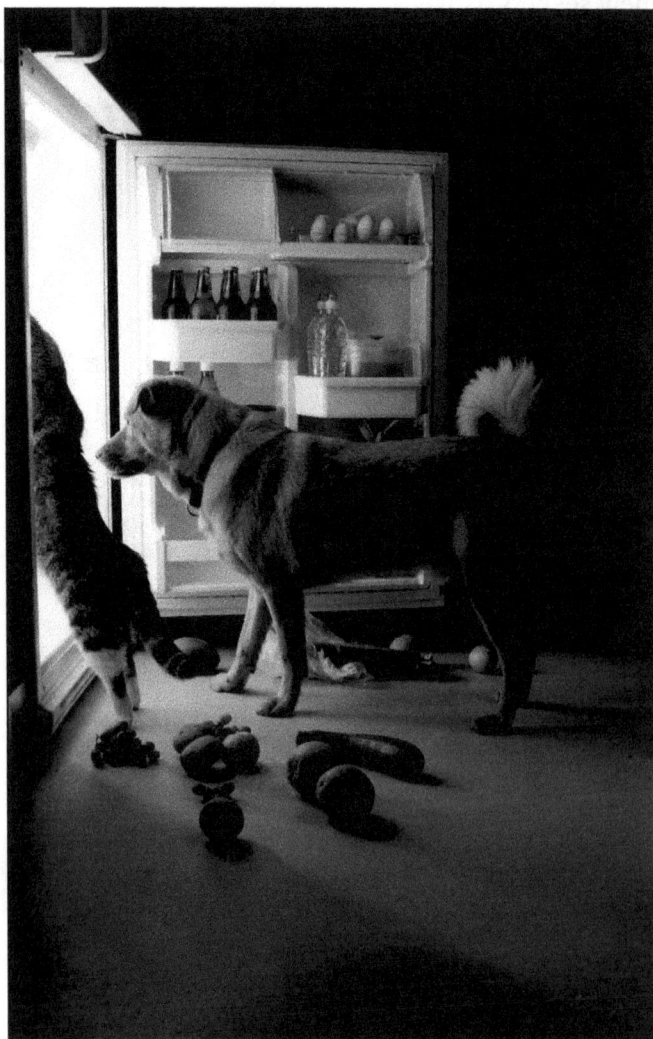

CHAPTER 6
The Food Situation

Even during a pandemic, we still need to eat, and to try to eat as healthy as possible. The same is true with our dogs.

Unfortunately, as the pandemic has progressed, in some parts of the country it has become increasingly difficult to get certain pet food brands or to even find pet food at all.

My dog Fletcher is fed a raw diet, and with meat and chicken plants shutting down, I have had trouble getting the meat staples I normally give him as part of his regular diet, such as chicken backs, liver and gizzards. Meats that are available have skyrocketed in price. Because of that, I've had to change his diet temporarily so that he's now fed a high quality kibble in the morning and raw for his evening meal.

What if your kibble isn't available and you have to switch to a new brand? First, try to find a similar formula, with the same protein(s) you have been feeding. Compare the ingredients and buy a kibble with a similar list of ingredients. This way, you improve your chances that your dog won't have an adverse reaction such as skin allergies or an upset tummy when you feed him the new food. Change him over slowly if you can, by mixing the two kibbles together in his food bowl.

One thing to avoid during any sort of crisis is to panic and buy kibble in bulk. Unlike toilet paper, kibble goes bad and often goes bad quickly. Most pet food companies won't tell you how long the nutrients in kibble will last – they don't want you to know.

The older the bag of food is, the more it has degraded and the greater the risk of contamination by bacteria and other toxins. Ideally, you should use any bag you purchase within 30-days of opening the bag.

The only time it's OK to stockpile food for your dog is if he's fed a raw or cooked diet, you have abundant freezer space, and aren't at risk of losing power for several days.

Yes, You Can Feed Table Scraps!

Being in the dog business for many years, I often hear the comment from dog owners "Oh I would never feed my dog table scraps or people food!" My response is "Why not?" As long as your diet is fairly healthy and nutritious, there's no reason why you can't give your dog some tasty leftovers. However, if your diet consists primarily of fast food take-out, please don't give your dog any. I've known people who reward their pup by giving them a burger from the local drive through fast food joint. Not a good idea!

On the other hand, whenever I make salad, which is almost daily, my dog Fletcher patiently waits for the crunchy ends of the lettuce spine. Romaine is his favorite! He always gets a bit of leftovers from most of what I eat, unless it's spicy. I save the skin from grilled salmon and other fish for him. He loves white bean soup. The list goes on.

The only caveat in giving your dog healthy table food is that you must account for that in his daily caloric intake. If he gets some table scraps daily, cut back on his kibble some. Otherwise, you'll eventually notice him putting on the pounds.

What to do if You Can't Afford Your Dog's Food?

What happens if you can't afford pet food at all? Call your local rescue organizations. Many have set up programs to help feed pets right now. They all want pets to stay in their homes, instead of being surrendered.

In many areas of the country, the ASPCA has set up temporary food distribution centers through support from various foundations, such as PetSmart Charities, and the Petco Foundation.

When we need them so much, now is not the time to have to even think about the possibility of surrendering your beloved pet because you can't afford to feed them.

If rescues aren't able to help, ask friends and neighbors for help. Put out a post on Nextdoor or a similar app. I think you'll be surprised at kindness and generosity of strangers, especially now.

CHAPTER 8
Your Dog and Your Children during Lockdown

One thing I'm sure of is that our dogs aren't used to spending so much time with our kids. Pre-pandemic, our kids were off at school or daycare, and while at home were busy playing with the neighbors, doing schoolwork, hanging out with friends, playing video games, and generally not spending a lot of time with the family dog.

Now, as even video games are becoming dull, children, especially younger ones, are looking for other ways to entertain themselves. This can involve your dog in positive and negative ways.

Because dogs have the emotional development of a young child, they also love to play. As dogs age however, their bodies aren't able to do what they used to (who can!) so play may become painful. No

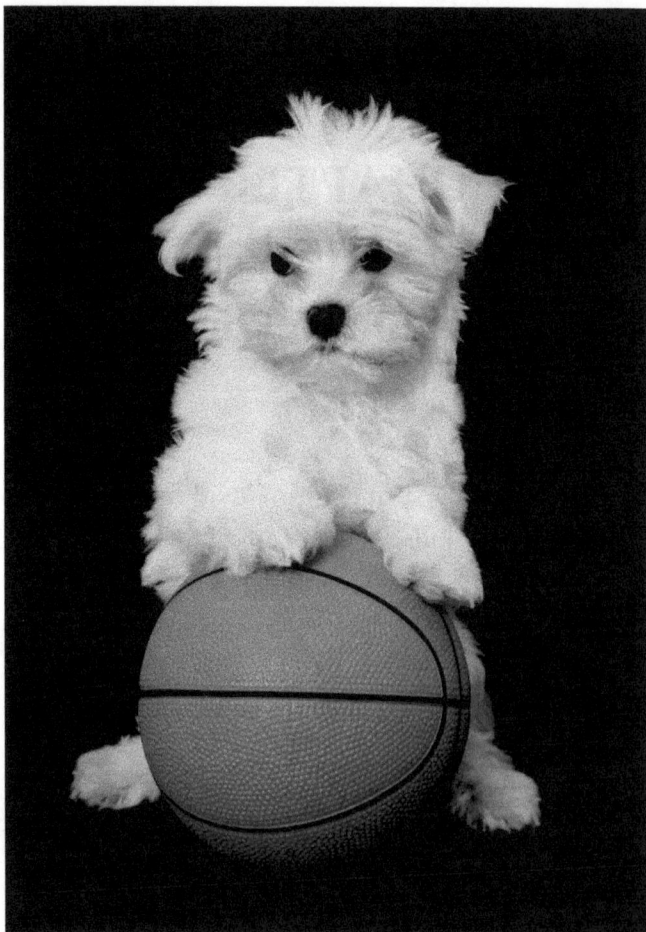

matter the age of your dog, you need to provide oversight any time your kids are playing with your dog. Make sure they aren't being rough, aren't teasing the dog, and ensure that your older dog isn't in any physical distress.

Supervision is Key!

Anytime your dog seems uncomfortable with what your children are doing with your dog, stop it immediately. Set boundaries for both your kids and your dog so they will both stay safe.

Unless a dog is completely shut down because of abuse, they always signal their distress via their body language in ever increasing ways, until their only choice is to bite. Unfortunately, most people don't recognize those signals, and as a result, many dogs are surrendered yearly because the owner says the dog "bit my child out of nowhere." That just doesn't happen.

Give your dog a quiet, private place to go to get away from your children when they need a break. This can be a room or a crate, but do not allow your children to enter this space while the dog is there. Also teach your children not to bother your dog when he is eating or sleeping.

Your Dog, You, and the Pandemic!

When your dog is done playing with your kids, and walks away, teach the kids to let him do that. He has had enough at that point, and as I'm sure many parents can relate, needs a break.

CHAPTER 9
Working from Home with a Playful Pup

If you regularly work from home like I do, no doubt you have a routine you follow with your dog that will allow you to get some work done. In my case, I have to make sure Fletcher is relatively well exercised in the morning so he'll nap and let me get some things done. If I don't do this, he'll think that it's my job to entertain him and I won't get anything done!

But if working from home is new to you because of the lockdown, I suspect your dog is doing a great job of trying to distract you from your job. It's likely that he's thrilled to have you around the house all the time and considers you his personal entertainment system now more than ever. It's also possible that he's bored or restless.

This is where exercise and mental stimulation become critical if you plan to keep the boss happy and complete your work.

If you can't get outside to exercise your dog so he'll leave you alone while you're working, give him some toys that will keep him busy and provide him much needed mental stimulation. Puzzle toys are a great way to keep your active pup busy. And they will wear him out!

Puzzle Toys for an Active Pup

Puzzle toys are the perfect solution to stimulate your dog's mind and improve his problem solving skills. They help your dog learn to focus as well as work to correct any behavioral issues he may have.

Puzzle toys can be introduced at any time in your dog's life. Start with simple toys, such as a frozen Kong that is stuffed with yogurt or almond butter then work up to more complicated interactive toys.

The beauty of puzzle toys is they can keep your dog occupied and help relieve boredom when you eventually do go back to work and he's back to being alone all day. Just make sure you select toys that are safe, can't be destroyed, and don't have parts that could become a choking hazard.

If you are able to get outside for some fresh air and exercise, do that periodically during the day whenever you can. Take your dog for a morning walk before beginning your work day. Take a late morning or lunch time break and go outside for a game of fetch or some other activity. Take your regular afternoon or early evening walk.

And remember while you're working to stop every now and then, look up from the computer, and give your best furry friend a pat on the head when he comes to visit you!

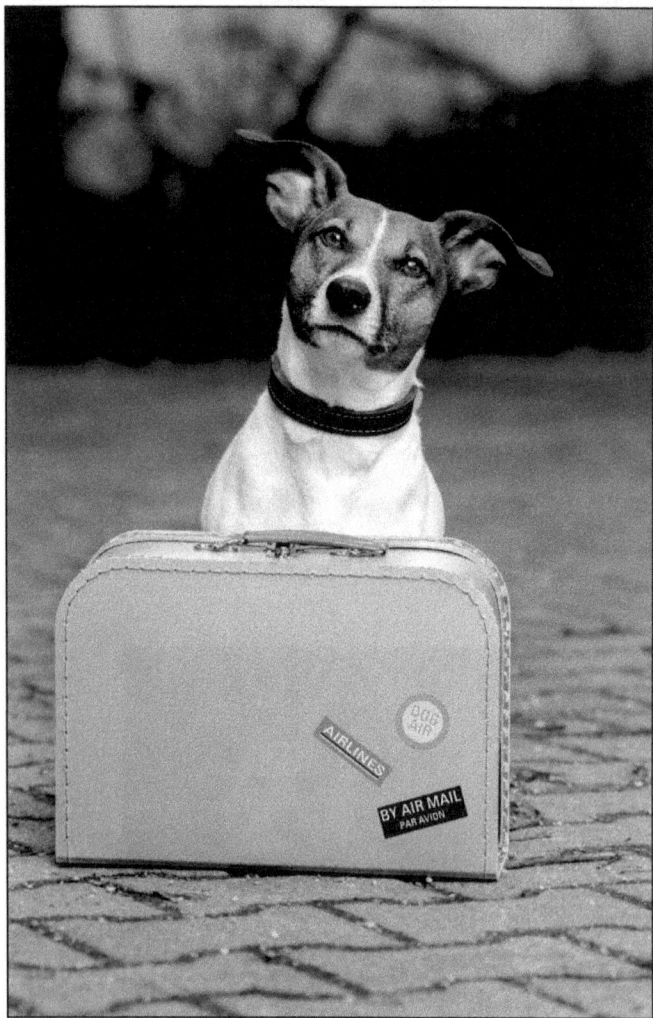

CHAPTER 10
Should You Adopt during a Pandemic?

As you're sitting home getting more bored each day, perhaps you've given thought that this might be a good time to adopt a dog.

Many people have, in part because of our need for companionship and comfort in an era of lockdown orders and social distancing. Many rescue organizations throughout the country have seen a large increase in the number of adoptions due to the pandemic. Foster applications are at an all-time high.

What to Consider Before Adopting

Before you rush out to adopt that cute puppy or older dog, there are a number of things you must take into consideration in making this decision. The pandemic won't last forever, but adopting a dog is a commitment to give him a home for the rest of his life.

- How much time will you have to devote to caring for the dog, post-pandemic? Dogs need training, attention, and regular exercise. If your normal life requires you to be away from home for long periods of time, perhaps you should reconsider or adopt an older dog that spends the majority of his day snoozing.

- Can you afford a dog long term? Dogs need food, regular veterinary care, toys, and more. You also have to plan for unexpected expenses you may incur.

- What about your housing situation? Do you rent or own? How much space do you have? The answers to these questions will determine if you should adopt, and if so, what size and age dog you should consider.

- Look at your lifestyle post-pandemic to determine what age and breed or breed mix would suit that lifestyle. If you're a runner for instance, look for a younger, higher energy dog. If you lead a more sedentary life, consider a breed more known to be a couch potato.

Socialization is Key

The downside to adopting a puppy or even a fearful dog during a lockdown is the inability to socialize him properly. You also won't be able to attend group training classes. Socialization is critical, especially for puppies and proper training is necessary throughout your dog's life. Training is not difficult to do at home; there are a ton of books and online videos that will teach you how to train your dog if you don't know how.

The plus side to adopting during this pandemic is the amount of time you'll have to bond with him while under lockdown orders. And you'll have a lot of time to work on training.

The key to a successful adoption is preparing your new dog for life after the pandemic. This is where routine is critical. Do your best to feed and walk him at the same time each day. If you're normally out of the house five days a week, plan to leave your dog home alone some now to prepare him for when you'll go back to your normal schedule.

Also consider investigating dog daycare facilities in your area if you end up adopting a social dog or a puppy. Find a good one and plan on enrolling your dog for at least one day a week, post-pandemic. This will help with his socialization and give him some much needed exercise while you're away for the day. Even though I work from home, I'll occasionally take my dog Fletcher in for a day of daycare, because he enjoys it. His best friend Henry however, hates going to daycare, and the only time he goes is when his mom has to be out of the house for longer than five hours.

Whatever you decide, please remember the commitment to this new life you are bringing into your home. Animals are thinking, feeling, sentient beings and are not disposable!

CHAPTER 11
Our Dogs and Life
After a Pandemic

At some point, life will return to some sort of normalcy, likely different than before the pandemic, but I'm certain we will return to work and school. What happens to our dogs then, after they've become so used to us being home with them all the time?

Over the generations, dogs have been bred to bond with humans, and today, they rely on us for almost everything – love and affection, attention and playtime, feeding, and more. They also love being around us. I imagine most dogs are thoroughly enjoying all this extra time we are spending at home with them. It's good for us as well, especially if we live by ourselves, to help ease the stress of isolation and provide that companionship and affection we all need.

Coping with the New Normal

When we finally do return to our normal daily routine, many dogs will have difficulty coping with this change, after becoming so used to having us around all the time. Dogs who do will likely show varying signs of separation anxiety. Symptoms can include shaking, drooling, whining, barking or howling when left alone. They can also exhibit destructive behaviors, such as chewing drywall or around the door.

Extreme behaviors can include dogs trying to escape through a window or any other type of opening, even if it's closed. I've actually known dogs who have crashed through glass windows to get out, because of their severe separation anxiety.

Easing the Transition

One way to ease your dog's transition back to your pre-pandemic routine is to leave the house each day if you can, leaving your dog home alone. This can mean going for a walk without your dog, doing some yard work, even going for a drive.

Your Dog, You, and the Pandemic!

Get dressed, put on your shoes, grab your car keys, and leave the house for a while. This way, your dog will remember that your departure is part of the normal routine. To make it even easier, give your dog a treat when you leave. This way, he'll associate your leaving with something pleasant.

Whenever I leave my home, I toss pieces of kibble on the floor in various areas for my dog to find. While I work from home normally, he used to get stressed whenever I left the house and didn't take him with me. Doing this small act has made it fun and rewarding to him, and I come home to find a calm dog and no damage to my home!

Find what works for you so your dog eases back into normalcy as best as he can.

APPENDIX
Books and Other Resources

The books and resources I've listed here are some of my personal favorites. I am a proponent of positive, force free training, and natural health, so I look for those when recommending and purchasing books. Most of the books listed here I have in my own library.

Training and Behavior

"Perfect Puppy in 7 Days: How to Start Your Puppy Off Right" Dr. Sophia Yin, DVM

"How to Behave So Your Dog Behaves" Dr. Sophia Yin, DVM

"The Power of Positive Dog Training" Pat Miller

"The Other End of the Leash: Why We Do What We Do Around Dogs" Patricia McConnell

"Love Has No Age Limit-Welcoming an Adopted Dog into Your Home" Patricia McConnell, Karen London

"From Fearful to Fear Free: A Positive Program to Free Your Dog from Anxiety, Fears, and Phobias" Dr. Marty Becker, DVM, Mikkel Becker, Lisa Radosta

"On Talking Terms With Dogs: Calming Signals" Turid Rugaas

"Canine Body Language: A Photographic Guide Interpreting the Native Language of the Domestic Dog" Brenda Aloff

The Association of Professional Dog Trainers

Certification Council for Professional Dog Trainers

Choosing a Great Dog Trainer 101 – AKC

Health and Nutrition

"The Nature of Animal Healing : The Definitive Holistic Medicine Guide to Caring for Your Dog and Cat" Dr. Martin Goldstein, DVM

"Dr. Pitcairn's Complete Guide to Natural Health for Dogs & Cats" Dr. Richard Pitcairn, DVM

"Four Paws, Five Directions: A Guide to Chinese Medicine for Cats and Dogs" Dr. Cheryl Schwartz, DVM

"Healing Touch for Dogs: The Proven Massage Program" Dr. Michael W. Fox, DVM

"Canine Nutrigenomics - The New Science Of Feeding Your Dog For Optimum Health" Dr. Jean Dodds, DVM

"Healthy Dogs, Your Loving Touch" Sherri Cappabianca

The Aromatic Dog - Essential oils, hydrosols, & herbal oils for everyday dog care: A Practical Guide Nayana Morag

Whole Dog Journal – A subscription magazine that provides a complete guide to natural dog care and training.

The Morris Animal Foundation

Animal Health Foundation

Hemopet

Dog Breeds

"The Complete Dog Breed Book, New Edition" DK Books

"The Dog Encyclopedia: The Definitive Visual Guide" DK Books

American Kennel Club

ABOUT THE AUTHOR

Sherri Cappabianca holds multiple certifications in small animal massage, as well as certifications in small animal acupressure, aromatherapy for animals, and canine hydrotherapy. She is also a 6th generation Reiki Master in the direct lineage of Usui, Hayashi, Takata, Gray and Rosenthal.

A lifelong dog lover, Sherri opened her canine health and wellness business, Rocky's Retreat in 2006, named after her golden retriever, Rocky, the special soul who inspired her on this path, and began working part time massaging dogs. After more than 20 years as a software engineer, she left corporate America in 2009 and began working full time with dogs, focusing primarily on their health and wellbeing.

In 2011, she joined forces with her new business partner to open Rocky's Retreat Canine Health & Fitness Center, located in Orlando, FL.

The emphasis was on hydrotherapy, having the only indoor warm water pool in Florida, massage, nutrition, behavior, and other healing therapies for dogs. Through the years, Sherri has helped countless dogs in the central Florida area recover from numerous health issues, lose weight, and have an overall better quality of life for a longer period of time.

Sherri also created a canine hydrotherapy certification training program through the Rocky's Retreat training arm, The Canine Fitness Institute. Through that program, she successfully taught hydrotherapy skills to hundreds of people throughout the country and Canada who have gone on to open their own successful hydrotherapy businesses.

In 2017, after building the business and deciding it was time to slow down a bit, they sold Rocky's Retreat and The Canine Fitness Institute and relocated to the beautiful mountains of western North Carolina.

Not wanting to retire, Sherri's focus now is on manufacturing raw and cooked foods for dogs, under the brands Canine Harvest and Lucky Dog Raw. Understanding the importance of quality foods for people and dogs, ingredients are sourced from local farms and ranches, which also helps to support the local community and economy.

Sherri continues to research new ideas on healthy dog care, give advice to dog owners, and write books about dogs from her home in Hendersonville, NC, where she lives with her Goldendoodle / lab / Irish wolfhound mix, Fletcher.

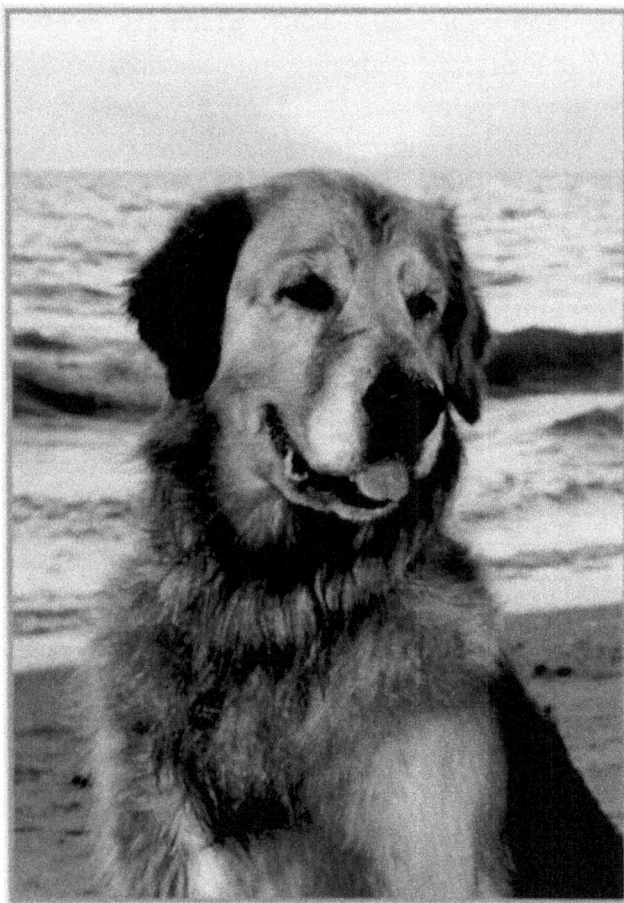

Rocky, my inspiration.

Ordering Information

All of Sherri's books can be ordered from any of the various online booksellers, and are also available on the Off The Leash Press website, offtheleashpress.com.

Your Dog, You, and the Pandemic!

www.ingramcontent.com/pod-product-compliance
Lightning Source LLC
Chambersburg PA
CBHW071735020426
42331CB00008B/2044